i

c

o

p

e

For more information, find CCM & Writ Large Press at:
http://writlargepress.com
http://copingmechanisms.net

to afar

from afar

BY SOHAM PATEL

Contents:

Proem

each and every

     one of you has a warfare

blooded artery

They will move they will have to move and you will move on them.
                                        -Theresa Hak Kyung Cha

You can melt brush like wax; and birds in time
Can sing.

                                        -Jack Spicer

Where you are going.   To offspring your own place
for the compass needle to point— make your own
magnetisms.   Only movement generates equations.
The push and the pull.   You carry a globe around:
furniture.   Used to reference, instruct, daydream,
decorate.   Ecliptic obliquities solve some loss.
Trace the figure eight. Follow the way the analemma
draws the path the sun makes in the sky. Memorize
the Equation-of-Time: *in the Northern Hemisphere if you
see the sun's position is more east than where the dial on your
watch says it would be, the Equation-of-Time is negative*—
the clock is behind the sun—*if the sun is more west, the
Equation-of-Time is positive*—the clock is in front of the
sun.   It will tell you what month.   It shows us the sun's
declination for every day in the year. You can sit still
feel the hours turn.

Sunlight on any piece of concrete
is one part whoever is walking.
One part fog on windows. Stew
of onions fried to red. The part
you cannot see is further east
in tobacco fields where workers
walk on to ruminate and roll what
will be smoked. To fasten leaves
with knots of thin pink string. All done
by foot and hand. One part is the tiger
cub knowing where the river water
is clean and can quench her thirst.
Know how the shadow holds suspicion
inside all these places. And noise
strands in lowland watersheds. Don't
forget the part the clouds bring.
On roadsides some mother
voices say—*none of this can bear
beginning.* The sunlight down
on any piece of ground is hope fathers
keep when they have to leave home.

This is to inform you:

You always wake up on the floor with a sore back. Look up and see your cousin's clean feet. She is on the bed sleeping. You start to sweat. Reach your hand up. Tickle her dirtless toes. *I was dreaming about your dad.* You say this to your cousin and her brother who is sleeping next to her. *I dreamed about him again.* Your cousin-brother rolls over and curls toes to ask. *Was he dead or alive?*

Both. He bought me an ice cream and a bloody beer, and then he shot me a few times. And then he shot himself.

A Saturday at the end of September—
You have slept through the morning.
Summer hangs on in an eighty-degree afternoon.
Mosquitoes woo mosquitoes in high pitch near your ear.

*Should we wake up you think and see if this heat won't kill
us? I don't want no ice cream or beer.* Your cousin-sister still
somewhere in the bardo. *Did you hear the rickshaw crash in
the night? I heard a lady scream,* you say, *I thought it was a cow.
That might have been when I finished my drink and your dad
first shot me in the mouth.*

Your cousin-sister is in your grandmother's nightgown. Lying and sweating under a cream colored cotton stamped with mahogany paisleys and flower petals.

Your cousin-brother stretches up his arms. Cheeks puff out as he exhales. Clean feet. *I saw a rickshaw hit a cow one time.* Each night he sleeps in the shirt from your uncle's soldier suit.

You are late for the tobacco fields.
You are to be making tea for uncles in them.
Women with babies tied to their backs
tear–sweat–sigh above perfuming leaves.
Your mustaches catch beads of sweat when you drive
the white Impala to your field after you shower. Have
your own tea. Walk to temple. Take off your sandals.
Circle the gods lodged there. Chant their mantras.

*I dreamed there was a cobra in the car. She was sleeping and you sat your bum
down*

    on her.

You stretch and sweat and swat at the air by your ears. You stand up first. Look with your cousin-brother out the window towards the field. The fan creeks the humid air in through iron bars onto your skin. You fix your squint by putting both hands over your forehead and curling your fingers to a cone for better sight—handmade binoculars for your eyes. You need glasses.

The southwest is bringing rain today.

You drag the straw mat off the floor
where you were sleeping—
dreaming of uncle killer.
You look to see if your cousin-sister has moved.

Give off, she says with her eyes still closed,
or I'm gonna give you a snake bite
in the bum for buggin' me all morning.

This is to inform you:

Because you stomach the push and have to smolder out
the glow at the end.

The landscapes dwell here in permanent recall. Shift
to drift the tectonic replay.

This is an apology for our mothers:

Only when the papers needed to be sent today. When we need to buy stamps.

When the visa application. Find the records. State. Where were you born.

The passport photos need to be taken. Immunization shots. Proof. Stamped.

Find someone to write your sponsor letter. Sign it. Find tickets. Find.

But you are proud and you and you and you.

Wait only in ghost to know we will remain.

Sound to the noise you've left for assurance.

Sound to throwing ceramic gifts

From the wedding at the wall behind his head. He ducks. Makes a puff.

Acoustic creature

Mapped by you. Songs try

To put us to sleep

But we were never tired.

Teeth grind under what you say between the driver's

Side window while you pass us on the freeway. We are
leaving. You are.

Ready for us to move you out. Tired of the questions

    You want your own life now.   This U.S. city
                                   by the bay.

Because every mother dies and everything changes.

Because every grandmother.

Because of every month we sleep in your wombs.

Because the milk was never sour   even
when from your bruised over nipples.

Because some girls practice to be you   to put
to sleep with each rocking hum.

Because tongues and blood atoms formed from one
ground here. From this air.

(Born here of parents born from parents the same, and
their parents the same).

Because every whispered promise in a hungry child's
birthday party.

Because we wear shiny cardboard cone hats to celebrate.

Because helium filled balloons tied with ribbon rise-pop-
fall to eternity.

Because we all have been naked and swimming. Naked
and dancing.

Because Your mother's soul hovers ahead.

Because we hover inside. We hover behind.

Because you travel with us and you are our companion.

Camel switch to a dictator's face. Mustached despot.

Who has a dream. Who wants you out. Who wants a
knife at father's head

Before the auspicious event is to be announced?   You are
on your way. Out.

Soldiers sing and laugh and load you on a bus. The end of a gun
Or a penis pushes up against the small of your back. You
leave each brother behind.

Because we're only wearing your shadow under cilantro
tomato mix.

Wish cumin. Wish lemon. Wish us here. Together after all.

This is to inform you:

Perhaps you too will call
on the eternal eye watching
down on the heady gestures
of our narrative—fading.
You ask for more time
or for at least an imaginable
land to live in. You wake.
Ask for quiet. The hammock
rocks and holds you like dust
lifted from under a blanket.
Trade each skin flake
for remembrance and lung sacs.

This is to inform you:

What we're told when we're put to sleep
sounds like a lesson, a lullaby rock,
a humming reference to keep careful to.
Bone depths of cologne soap ignite in din—
light fire to warm to calm for the deities.

How to make a good husband.
How to make a good wife. How
to make all the children obey
right. To make a house hold run.

Flames are the place from which you came.

Clouds are simple cousins to the elephants
that could fly.
Don't leave the house without first eating
something sweet.
Drink at least a sip of water before you go.
Shoes off at the door as you enter.

Left hand logic
is right handed

—the right hand is
cleaner than the left.

If you dangle your feet while sitting on the swing, your parents will die.
Sleeping on your stomach will make your backside grow fat.
When lizards watch you in the bath, you'll know the rain is coming soon.
If the lizard falls onto your lap, wealth will come too. On a gold chain
wear an elephant's tooth around your neck, it will bite and hold your anger.
When a dog cries outside your bedroom window at night that's
when you know

someone you love is going to die.

Bathe at day's break.
Dirt accumulates.
Don't cut your finger-
nails after dark.

This is to inform you:

In the head, blood
rushes and stings
parts of our faces,
to teach
us where not to make wrinkles, he says.

There is no mention
of your brother's last
sent letter from home.
And the torn photo.

All the wives
and moms and dads
and sons and daughters
get their standard reply—

★

Uniformed men on front
steps. Regret folded flags.

You press hard
against vinegar
soaked tongues

and draw a map of Chinatown
on the dirt dusted sidewalk
with the sole's toe end of your black
canvas and white rubber sneakers.

—you skin maroon at any season's start.
No electricity from the grid to make the ceiling fan spin.
Just gaze at the layer of gray dust puffing up
from ends of each angry painted blade wanting to cut
the air. You are afraid to try and wipe it clean because you
see the whole thing is only held up by a single, fraying wire.

If daydreams could
complete sentences,

the portrait in the attic
would have a story to tell.

You would hear versions both
with coordinates, subordinates.

she is your grandmother   she was
a good woman   she

Everyone says. Everyone stares
somewhere on the marble floor

or into the muggy enough
to put you back to sleep air.

The woman in the photograph—
bone thin with no smile - looking

straight into the camera - her
long long fingers gloved over

a tapestried table - might
have a song to play you.

The photo is black and white
her skin is what color.

Her rings wink back at the camera's flash.
The flowers on the table appear to be

north and south and east and western—
petals are sharp cutting wings

or thick circles round in bloom.
A harmonium on the floor

just near her feet.
Her portrait sits

dusty in the top most room of this mountain
granite and concrete gray rising bungalow.

When you were a little boy
you would go to the top story

every afternoon while the others
slept together downstairs on the floor.

Everyone sleeps   it helps them forget
the heat   you can't eat when you sleep.

You always wake up hungry.
Your pale red cricket ball

and the humming of old
movie tunes keep you company.

They say you came from a long
line of daydreaming musicians

who never studied music—
only listened with ears

so open to the entire earth
melodies could crawl in

break their hearts and on
their way out rapture

bodies with ecstasy enough
to make an idea   an idea

anyone could return to if
ever it became necessary.

At one time you believed the stars were cousins to dog howls   that the wind in the leaves is what gives birth to car horns sounding on the horizon.

On an other note:

A familiar smell hit. You lit a cigarette. Lungs ache.
Exhale and the smell becomes a memory of a cousin who
stole bidis one by one, then two by two, then pack by
pack from an uncle's cabinet. You both smoked in the
summers on the roof where yellow-green lizards and roti-
thief monkeys live.

Watch other children fly kites from other rooftops every
morning before you brush your teeth.

Wake up around midnight and it is raining. You soaked red
lentils in a pot since before the morning. Put the pot on a
burner set to high heat. In another pot pour oil then
it goes on the burner set to medium heat. Each will need
45 minutes. Pour wine and pull a yellow onion from a
basket. Papery flakes fall on the floor. You leave them there.
Chop and drink and let tears clean your face. Drop in
cumin seeds. They sizzle they dance.
Onions, more cumin, lemon, tomato, red powder, yellow
powder, salt and honey get spooned into the hiss.

Combine what is in the two pots into one bowl and put
it aside. Go to the porch. Smoke in the rain before you go
back to sleep.

You dream you have a job. It is to find one of Emily
Dickinson's books. The library at your old school. You
have to run to get to it on time. You have to run now. Find
it on a windowsill under the stone-carved cherub who
peers down nosed in his own book. Pick up the book you
found. See it is a J.D. Salinger novel instead. Dickinson
is in the binding of what you hold in your hands.

Crack the binding's glued brown leather and wood. The
pages are flimsy. They crinkle, are almost translucent.
You touch them. They turn into white wings and fly out
of the building. You have to run again. You are chasing
the wings. Catch them near the rose bushes. Pinch down
on the wings with your fingertips. They ignite. Smoke
flies. The wings become orchid petals.

On an other note:

City walls have of course given birth to the clinic
where the limits of recourse furnish ephemeral fashions
like desire. A place for old reality-a place as ancient as
globalization-is given back. Traded spice for the nubile—
jewels for the sunset.

Travelers cannot hide the money where they are coming
from, so they say prayers for each breakfast eater tonight.
To hang dresses over balconies—cotton promises to keep
cool. All in the colors dyed to know how to soothe any
ideas thrown as sighs and saying anyway.

As for the wayward dwellers, they'll spill salt when you
start sweating curry spice from oil pores. Take
the seashells to the painter. They take your name down
in tiny Arabic letters. You have taught them well.

There is no solitude. Everyone is the noise on the streets
succeeding the passive pensive beings who lurk smiling
toothless in corners. We'd give this language a heart if we
could only minimize the egg, eliminate the skin, distance
the thought of grammar from dust.

Undeliverable letters returned to sender pile up on the
floor inside. The color of rain on the city paints ways to
embrace any silent gaze. Gray on concrete and the green
leaves outside. Embrace like the fire in the corner of the
room. Cold anywhere but here. The light is fixed so
come to know the sound of a shawl drying in the wind.
Write me by the firelight and when you walk outside
at night, forget the wind carved cliffs on which you are
living. After days of falling, climb back to the top. Fall off
again. The cars below. Whatever stayed the same must
have been wrong. Wheels are stuck at go. Horn buzz
and your unheard song. Sand between toes and always
your questions remind you to cry. How can distance be
measured with outdated stamps? Keep every shiny bit of
paper that ever wrapped your gifts in shoeboxes under
your bed. Hibiscus falls and you bend. It brings me to
my knees. Hold my hands when we walk at dusk down
stairs the workers cut out of the cliff on its way up from
the beach. If the sun rises in time, I'll follow you brightly.
In the body you breathe the arch of diaphragms pushing
intercostal muscles and both lungs into remembered
shapes. Hold the breeze over. Hold it in. Count to ten.
Slowly. Then let it out. Edges sweep sharp. The dull
blade of a letter opener through licked paper and glue.

gun metal moon shine
turns some grief into action
while tides come and go

Wind–ripped tarp dangles blue from the houseboat rooftop. Knotted at the center. Banana leaf rope. A jar almost full of dead yellow jackets. Out goes the fire lamp so attraction ends for the scout. The queen's buzz-buzz army will recollect under the wind-ripped knot until dawn.

Morning raga opens a red harmony and breaks down
the net. Sound the warnings.
The boatman wheezes through his nose. Bugs crawl.
Some fly. The rope is frayed. Eaten.

We wake sooner than the sadhu who howls slim when he sees the sun. [it is not shining]. [he's been stoned and knows we know this]. The light washes. Your circuitry stops. Is the sadhu-howl causing you to sweat? For a moment we interpret the percussion's ending.

There are smiles. Hand pats on backs. A taxicab comes.

In the waiting room. The lights buzz and the interns
laugh off what they do not know yet.
Sleeping men and cats in the hallway spell out where
the line is to pay before treatment.

We see no tables full of magazines with photos from
around the world. No water machine.

The fishermen :: guides to a new inland.
The boats :: homes for spirit hunters.
The temple bells :: like mosquito flight near our ears.
There are no nets in the backwater night.
There has been another strike :: The workers.

Our soundings turn to mirth
and we remember the moment
that began this openness, this breath.

Entire undoings bite down on finger skin. Sand follows us everywhere. The floor rumbles like lament. Diamonds on hand. The piercing. Head. Lapped up in a lap of silence. Shine and dog paw. Birdprints. Dust and crumbs.

Transparent wings about to be carried away by a band of bees.

You tell me you are home and you
are not home yet. Come to drown
the name of that boy. The eyeless

one sitting on temple stairs. Carve
his name into the mosque's walls.
In the churchyard alone. Take

my name down with you. Swell
a harmony with the surging stream
so each sound together might

put you back to sleep. The boy
broke some laws. He could not read.
You were the soldier—told

to help him upon your arrival.
He stole your chewing gum.
You keep on singing his song.

Midnight, your
birthday. Your father
sent a roll of quarters.
We can go do laundry
or walk on down
to the bar/arcade.
The moon is a riot.
Colors come down
like curtains.
Silver. Orange. Blue.
The radio stays awake
with old college rock
tunes. Call in, request
your favorite song. What
language? OK means zero
killed. The soldiers say
it is so on other radios.
The barracks shape up
like dorm rooms do.
Smelling of socks, how
some boys do—
oh, boys – oh, boys.
We skipped over cracks
on the sidewalk. We've
got our mothers' backs.

On an other note:

A breeze mixed with sun
sends the white plastic
shopping bag afloat.

What was in it is gone—
a blessing
from this pale heat.

A red thread ties itself around
your unmarried right wrist. You wait.

Blue air drops on the train tracks.
Sound is made like a friend's last lyric.

Torn and burning. Toes curl under the bench.
Chase the shade. Make a refuge for the blue air.
Now one can hear the last lyric loudly.

Cadence from your
sniffle lets late afternoons groan
out fresh pangs from each empty car.

Winter jasmines
creep in
the bloom of morningscent.
It has been another Sunday
of the hour-after-hour-waking-eating-sleeping.
All the fruit in the basket.
Translated and skimmed headlines.

Pillow, window light, an astir reflection of your voice.
The milk sweet dish   mother sent by mail.
Taste is balanced with black tea and hot sour pickle.
The metal gate creaks. Lie down and pretend—
these sounds are me whispering in an entrance.

All that's missing
are the keys to the safe in which you keep some
guns and all my correspondence.

The subsonic sigh of your wanting
        has been the only visible thing allowed
                into this dog cry and cricket song lit night.
It lets me see how that darkness lingering above
                your tongue is hairline cracked to let a little light in.

Even the angels have kept the cold in this night
                                for their desolation rituals
        at the hand of holding their hands over their
        mouths and tired ears.

Now sleep away
        and take only our parting with you.

U.S. BIPLANE
BEGINNING SCOUTING FLIGHT OVER MEXICAN BORDER
PHOTO © UNDERWOOD & UNDERWOOD N.Y.

POST CARD

THIS SIDE FOR CORRESPONDENCE

THIS SIDE FOR ADDRESS

Postage Stamp
Here

Domestic
One Cent
Foreign
Two Cents

PUBLISHED BY AMERICAN COLORTYPE CO., CHICAGO

NO. 5.

The Mexican trouble proved of considerable value to our army as a practical training field in which to try out the efficiency of the several arms of the service. Here our aeroplanes were put into use for scouting purposes, and from the service they saw down there, the Aviation Corps learned a great deal regarding the demands that would be made on them in actual warfare, and just how their equipment could be improved. Our aviators have won from the cavalry their right to the title "the eyes of the army," and are demonstrating to the world every day, their effectiveness in this field.

My mind goes on containing a great number of cities I have never seen and will never see, names that bear with them a figure or a fragment or glimmer of an imagined figure:

-Italo Calvino

i'll tap the wooden match out of its box

light it up on my shoe like cool filmy boys do

i'll burn each cigarette you bring to me duty free

in slow blows that say we can call-it-home here

wanderers—we do dear when there are wells turned dry

we will with wine or with an empty bucket

we will lift from the chairs we will sweat and tear

we will spry slick fix facemasks on for cold weather

you put cartons in the deep freeze so not to stale our draws away

you kiss me like a cigarette/two spotted cows on your breath

pull my burned fingertips in with your cracking knees

take   smolder   pinch all the butts   flick and flame again

did you see
the drone

Durga: the exit picture, a handle to a pull
down screen? She is in there—the   drone—paint on metal and plastic—a door
picture and the fractals as they touch everything → the supine like the summer
folding yes the summer   folds she says as women & gowns do—looking
funny like a cartoon   There's air—   float & sun a bit uncertain so close we
call it camaraderie   a ring—three   fly now   and here hover but if you could see
us—here you can   rings, fire &   and love and love and love let's fly away
on some foreign   country song or to the place where
she was born

There is a **Drug** *in your name*—**Durga.**

(Mother Durga flies while her tiger
 disturbs your float. Lion
     or Tiger—did she have
a favourite? TheTigerOrTheLion?
   in Soroti she said she was
never afraid of the tiger—
   childhood days—he said
they're so beautiful—but—but
the dogs for thirty seconds wrote
& read their names in the dirt—she
was afraid of dogs and last night
he said a German shepherd bit him
in the hand—one bit her in the back
once before but she's less scared now.

Cavalry comes—then we can debark so
she can walk down to touch the ground.)

I am near in the distance and far enough now. I am near enough to you.

There is no trainwreck—it makes no echo so if you hear it—hear it and forget.

There is no threshold to enter or exit. We know our boundedness. We pretend

that we never met. After you remember my name you feel the need to offer

me your neck but only at the places where your hair is too short to cover it.

We can leave any gate ajar. I have been sent here to join you. Here is a song

for you and all the dust we've left for each other wherever—
this is just a love song

to hum in your head as the men at our destination ask us for our
papers and you

show them your soldier suit and your suitcase and you give them,
also, your neck.

"And the sign says long haired freaky people need not apply."
You can't forget

that lyric while I cross the border with lice eggs hidden in my
head. Pretend

our belongings don't become quarantined upon our arrival. Stop
the offering

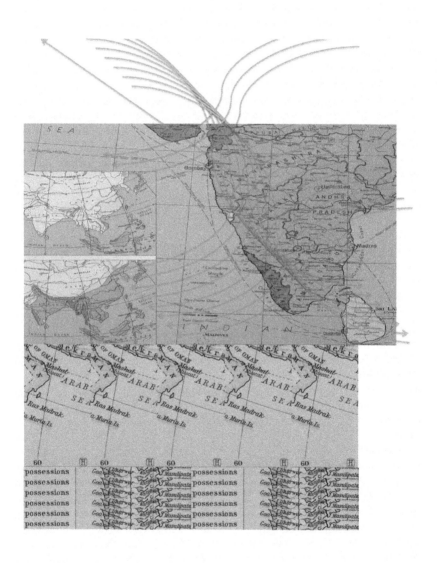

of apologies, of your lips, of your ticket, of your blue passport, offer

each language you can speak instead, even the ones you think you forget

how to say *excuse me* in, or *this is my destination, where is the hospital,* or *I love you.*

Wear chap stick when we kiss. Why can you understand me? Pretend

you don't speak English. Perspiration and tobacco tunes with a new song

and we sing it like desperateness—a body underneath another body,
we hear it

and we sing the wrong words at the wrong time. I laugh into your neck.

We smoke and drink whiskey until we fall into each other's laps. We pretend

we understand what bounds us. We hang your scarf on our train car. We forget

to hold on to health and vitality and happiness but remember this song:

We travel in search of nothing, so that we may achieve the intelligence of butterflies. You

know you should be alone so move on. And so I splinter. Break my head. Offer my own dust to the stars. What I forget to do is grieve us. I pretend

to understand now the veneer tones of Hello. How are you? I am fine. I neck

through strangers standing in a queue like it is just a matter of a sharp knife. You

understand that I made a plan in case you cannot come with me and I offer

that plan on a note pad now ink and sweat smeary. Words cheat us sometimes as song

to sway with, a way for us to think there is no need to splinter, as upshots in which to forget.

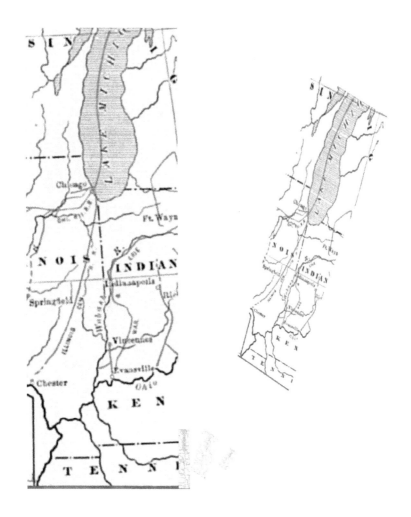

68

But contingency is a good tool for survival. Love is still
arriving and I did, I did forget your gait. I forgot your
recovery. I am certain we have not eaten in days. So I offer
a dressing for your wound, an occasion for return, an
occasion for wind, our song again. It rang in my head all
day and I heard it on a train. I can sing it from the neck
down to where we can communicate within great works. A
bilbliomancy of pretend I can come to you where you are,
offer your doormat's remains to the driver. Would you

have me cut your hair off then—stand in front of me, have me hold it all above your neck before I cut it? We could use that sharp knife for something else after—we could pretend you don't hate how long it takes to restore a body after travel. I have so much to tell you.

Rusted cartoon youth. Bent ears
and buck toothed. We are some
kind of epic. Resting in the shadow
of a dictator's face. After the partition—
he gathers his men up to flag you down.
Preambles of a well lit parade. The lengths
of black tea arriving, of currents. For what
are the distances the heart globes over?

The boarding school where your father
sent you allows one meal a day.
Your mother sends food. The food
never finds its way into your room.

★

It's time to let the planes fly
blow the whistle and begin to dig.
You left town for that southern
city where the radio fuzzes its
way too far south. But you
will return and we will dance well
-rhythm matches eyes-eyes match hips-
without any voltages or even any music.

Mixed with always:

When riding in your quick love wake, a changing light steadies itself, lets you learn how to read earth's geometry while reading your own.

A tremor is about to come. You'll let yourself be startled when fingers come to rub your lips just so to wake you up.

Tongues count moles and scars over all the resting bodies. Wind chants round your head, reminders.

You are too tired to be tranquil. You have burning eyes. All your clothes are still on. Put the book down. The sun is about to rise.

Mixed with always:

Suture rhythm stitches
stored dark in
a cool dry place
are mixed with always—
perhaps in the pages
of a memory book, perhaps
a place where
the townspeople
gather to hear
tones of warm
embrace, where we
reckon in the night.

You are the one who offers
the light. You, the one who
holds our bizarre passions,
who listens like fruit saved
in the ice box forgotten
and recalled years later.

We are listeners as well as speakers
Of this mystery, both of us,
But who else will join
This strange companionship?
~Jalāl ad-Dīn Muhammad Rūmī

Words continue to lift
memories off the page.
And measures are mixed
with the acoustics of breath.

When I want you here only when.
The smell of skin over sternum, you
wake to my exhales and cannot help
but want to sleep. Cannot ever
help just shining as morning eye light.
Cabin fire correlation. Wood
and menace about to burn into blue.
Stay until after the dawn.

Light for the faithful comes steadfast as rope
fray. As iron bars or stars. We've all felt
love before and so the light is nothing
new, always new. Instrumental and cryptic
as one-arm lunches. No dialogue—no
dialect. No screen towards another's face.
Uncertainty faces peace. Faces itself.
Concrete pours and dries in due equations-
of-time. We've all felt love before and so
the breaking of it is nothing now. Like
flower petals each fall, you detach.

You told me once: you said *Everything* to the casual
accosting of, "What's new?" Eyes all aflutter like the
longing you see on everyone's face. The light meat and
dark under our sockets differentiated only by the light.
Your fraying rope holding your trousers up. Your empty
stomach. The kind of empty that needs to be for the sake
of clarity. Like the love and the instruments we make in
our minds to make love, yes love, shine.

Lounge back with the steadfast
rope. See how
brown it is? It will keep you
dry if you need—
quiet share with the afternoon -
metaphors with no referent -
lovers with no face -
place for tears - a song to wake to -
the black dog
hugging you with his head -
benefit from unruly
hibernation – fast hunger
like a train wreck airing out
in the field you left behind.

In my paragraphs rest the difference between two
heartstrings and all the sores in your mouth. Between the
thud of your rebellion and the constitution that shadows
over your every endeavor. There are moth wings to
be eaten and even Elizabeth Taylor could play a saint's
mother just to show us how each role condones itself
as itself. A role. In time. Ends. Or the character's apex
forces decline - submits to the language of loss. Because
we've all felt love before and so the trembling delivery of
spontaneous *achu* is nothing new mixed with always new.

Synchronicity strikes the day your bible gets held for ransom.

When you leave home and can remain comforted is when

you know you have been forgiven.

Under meteoric skies—
songs ring to save you.

Jobs are made
as artificial loons

come lurching up
the spine of your gallantry.

Just before soldiers soak
        black rain   -   hearts beat.
           Arrowtargets end
   and moments
        speed up to stillness.

The pocketful of empty hands.
The engine. The road
edging with white lilacs to widen hand me-
                  down
gestures towards a tamer shoreline. No more war.

Days of rest,
          but never the newspapers:
  the color red reads
        in headlines   -   untimely deaths.
        Filled fractal adverts. Numb wound joy.

        Enemies: manufactured by the man.
Something to write home.

Fill in the blanks with a wanting eye.

What could have come

                was peace   -   a wind
  carrying the tune of a new
                  fruit budding.

River grows old. The last lion comes down to drink.
She walks alone in the early mornings. Grandmother
spoke closer by ink than she can by speech. Her found
stories written between the skins of her tabla. Tear it
apart. Need to see hollowness. Wait to hear her sing oh but
you ruined her instrument. Just a lullaby memory left.

Silver rains wash with morning
So I won't shine with the sun

Dream you never have to
walk to the river alone. Never
before sunrise. Lion cubs can swim
to mothers on other sides. Snakes, peacocks
cry like kittens. And the dogs. The moon floods
down to illuminate the end of night. Dream
until you are too afraid to leave the front
gate. No electric hums keep you awake.

So I won't shine with the sun
Silver rains will wash to dew

In musicality like the one you've salvaged there
are not enough proofs to map. Never histories
uncover. Passed down and out stories between
the villagers become lullabies to warn the children
into listening—into wanting nothing but quiet.
Mend the drum. Make the words up as you go.

Window rustle brings more
       light than comfort.
So cold the candle
wax drip holds all
       focus. Fingers
press in density
       of wick and burn.
Boiled water poured
in the kitchen
sink melts then
freezes the rubber plug
away from recognition.
Running. Freezing. Stop.
Stay awake and decide—
awake and deciding. How
to go back to sleep.

Mailman's been reading our postcards again.
Re-occurring messages from back east.
       Bedtime stories and night light endeavors from your lips.
A list of pictures piles up by your pillow:
       Sleek and green. Ocean under coral lens. Spray
       paint mosaics. Something like sepia.

You're the jazz sitting still in your leisure suite
       under a fan—white and dusty of course.
You sing tattoo songs like kings and queens might do.
They sting, are elegant, blood and scabs always rise.

Snippets of sleep poetry. Your children are everywhere else and here.
       You name a breeze. You have a satellite family.
       Postcards each week.
Everything's for safekeeping:
       Scraps of gift-wrap. Mid-wife maxims held under
       a blanket.

Receipts form piles so your pillow never holds alone.
On Monday morning, Mailman tells you reading so much
       in one sitting can't be good for the continuation of things,
tells you the date and to wake up—
       the world keeps coming and fiercely it waits again and again.

I point my heart straight at your eye. You study a globe. You draw
          maps. What travels at the speed of 39 cents per stamp?
There are no flames for the sky tonight
          though   its golden burns so bright, close enough to calm,
so you press repeat and rearrange the rest.

To vanquish—set forth on dreadful
expeditions. Know they are nothing
but tributes. For family. For nation:
      Out of food and moving on.
Thoughts of hauteur
      battle themselves between
daylight and sand grains break face skin.
Deserts beat like funk.
You think it is yours. You
do not know if you belong here now.
Warrior on. Camouflage beige
the idea of water—
      and breath.
Greed can't get you home.
It allures   every
myth you've ever
been assigned to read
into your tent at night
and takes each back
to its own basic folly
because chaos was never
only in the beginning.
Take a dollar everyday
you go to heaven.
Throw the rock up up up
up up and again.

—ubiquitous and proud—
live with whatever
divine and dormant power
lies in the confluence
of every stream ending in
the oceans. Deny no river.

Coalesce enemies and memories
stay in place with the confusion
that links system fervor. Return
home—there is where you'll be
told everything will be forgiven.
You're told everything will be OK.

Your songs
        are the impossible ruins
        that keep the hours on turn.
        Keep awe bare like
sound at night.
The candle burn. Ice
melts and wax. The dirt
on your mind. Engines roll
in clutter. Clank cool
and electrify the room.
We always
become mysterious—
birds at the end of each evening.
Whoever does the telling stops
time like a crescendo. We hit
blue notes so the edges
of your honey jars rattle laughter
against our teeth.
Rhythm breaks
like need or the knowledge
a mouth organ has
about breath and tone, blood
and gravity and balance—
all those sweet sounds
that can make even
windows shatter.

Mixed with always:

The bordello where you died
is now my attic apartment.

The landlord kept the old hex
bolts in the wood.

Every night – the airwaves
remind me you have won.

You have remained. You cradle
me as you cradled all the others.

Leave a piece of youth. Sentiment becomes
your friend again. I have been practicing

and tonight for the last time I will sing
you all the way to sleep. From then on

you will sing these lullabies to yourself.

As you trace your finger over
the globe your uncle gave you
the year you were born,
you remember how he used
to call it your baby earth.
It has raised and indented
relief. Your finger trembles
when you spin it fast. Fast
like the metals spinning
past the mantle at the core.
But on this 12" replica
of where we are—with its
white-like-parchment antique
ocean—only synthetic resins
and textile fibers can reside.
You remove a line of dust.
Rolling fingerwide waves.
Recall this isn't like those
go-where-your-finger-lands
when-the-spinning-stops
destiny kind of games.
This is for remembering
the dust trail you're always
leaving behind and the one
you aim at errantly
like a bewildered scout.
If language can only offer
a reduction of things—
why is it years
later when you notice
it still says Ceylon, you say
nothing and keep spinning?

★

Notes/Acknowledgements:

Some lines in This is to inform you: [Because you stomach the push...] come from Walt Whitman's "Song of Myself" and Paul Celan's "The Travelling Companion" translated by Michael Hamburger.

Postcard and map images are treated screenshots from various Internet searches.

The italicized line with the butterflies in the split sestina comes from a translated "Four Personal Addresses" by Mahmoud Darwish.

Photos are from my family's return to Soroti in 2016 after the 1972 expulsion of Asians from Uganda.

So much thanks to Oxeye Press for producing a handmade chapbook version of the smoke prelude—for now/in   airplane/to hear it and forget movement that appears here.

Grateful acknowledgements to the editors and publishers of the journals and anthologies where versions of the following pieces appeared:

Malleable Jangle   [Sunlight on any piece of concrete...]
Copper Nickel   [Because you stomach the push...]
                                [If daydreams could/complete sentences...]
Stirring Literary Magazine   [—you skin maroon at any season's start...]
DUSIE and Best American
Experimental Writing   [A familiar smell hit...]
                                [Just before soldiers soak...]
eleven eleven journal   [City walls...]
DesiLit Magazine   [Wind-ripped tarp dangles blue...]
The Cortland Review   [A breeze mixed with sun...]

Bull City Press' Another and Another Grind Anthology: [Midnight, your/ birthday...]
Achiote Press' Here is a Pen: An Anthology of West Coast Kundiman Poets: Hello, Ghost

Much gratitude to Western Washington University, University of Pittsburgh, University of Wisconsin in Milwaukee, to Kundiman, to Woodland Pattern, and to The Accomplices.

The most grateful of acknowledgements, too: to all of yous who know (you know) none of this could happen without.

OFFICIAL

CCM ◑

GET OUT OF JAIL
* VOUCHER *

- - - - - - - - - - - - - - - - - -

Tear this out.
Skip that social event.
It's okay.
You don't have to go if you don't want to. Pick up
the book you just bought. Open to the first page.
You'll thank us by the third paragraph.

If friends ask why you were a no-show, show them
this voucher.
You'll be fine.

- - - - - - - - - - - - - - - - - -

We're coping.

◑

9 781948 700016